T0107519

FIRED UP! EMPLOYEES

ARIC BOSTICK

iUniverse, Inc.
Bloomington

Fired Up! Employees

iUniverse books may be ordered through booksellers or by contacting:

iUniverse
1663 Liberty Drive
Bloomington, IN 47403
www.iuniverse.com
1-800-Authors (1-800-288-4677)

Cover design by Flip Design Studio, Inc.

Interior graphics by Düable Design & Development, LLC

Author photos by Kathy Whittaker Photography

ISBN: 978-1-4759-4354-2 (sc)
ISBN: 978-1-4759-4355-9 (e)

Library of Congress Control Number: 2012914330

Printed in the United States of America

iUniverse rev. date: 08/08/2012

This book is dedicated to all those who think they have lost their fire, but need to know it is still there.

This book is also dedicated to John Graeser—my confidant, my godfather, my friend. The words written here are just bite-sized pieces of the huge smorgasbord of wisdom you have graciously and selflessly bestowed upon me. Without you in my life, I am nowhere. Thank you with all my heart.

Contents

About the Author

Aric Bostick, one of the nation's leading motivational speakers and success trainers, has inspired and equipped more than a half million people from all walks of life to believe in themselves. By choosing to set higher goals and take action, Aric shows people how to choose and create a more fulfilling life. After experiencing his own hardships as a teen, Aric's mission became to guide people in overcoming their own personal challenges—using those experiences to ignite greater achievement and happiness. Ultimately, this inspires the mentorship of others.

Based on his latest book, *FIRED UP!*, Aric passionately introduces energy and performance to the workplace and beyond—blending humor, inspiration, and highly practical tips in his world-class keynotes and workshops. Aric is consistently a favorite speaker with corporations, associations, and schools. Visit **FiredUpEmployees.com**, or call 1-888-629-0179 today to learn how Aric can help your group become FIRED UP!

Acknowledgments

I want to thank my family, beginning with my father Jerry Bostick, who got me on the path of personal transformation at an early age; my mother Sue Isaac, who I love so much and has taught me so much; my brother Robbin Bostick, who has loved me unconditionally through all my ups and downs and provided me shelter and support when I needed it most; and my nephew Marty Bostick, who is my number one fan, and I am his.

Nancy, Mark, Haley, Gavin, Greg, Carla, Riley, Carson, Bennett, Tripper, Jennifer, Frank, Jack, Sam, Frankie, Reece, Whitney, and Christopher, thanks for being such great sisters, brothers, nieces, and nephews. I love you all so much!

Anne Bruce, thank you for seeing the light in me. You have given me so much inspiration. You are such an amazing woman, wife, mother, grandmother, and friend. Thank you for believing in me and giving me an opportunity to grow and expand and shine. Without your love, support, confidence, and constant reassurance, this book wouldn't have been written. Your input, contribution, and wisdom helped this book be what it is. YOU FIRE ME UP!

Phyllis Jask, thank you for your amazing energy, attitude, talent, and skill. I am blown away by how much better this book is because of you. You are FIRED UP!

Jocelyn Godfrey, thank you for jumping right in and helping us get this book done and making sure it was the absolute best it could be. Your help has been invaluable and I am so grateful you joined our team.

Michelle Lemons, thank you for believing in me, putting up with me, and always giving 100 percent to our work together. I am so blessed to get to work with such an amazing person. You have so many gifts and I am blessed by them every day. Thanks for taking me and what we do to the next level! You are AWESOME!

Susan O. Boyle, thank you for being my BFFEAE! Your unconditional friendship and ability to listen to me for countless hours as I blab about the minutia of my life have helped me change, grow, and become a better person. Our talks are the fruit of my life. They always leave me feeling better!

JeniLynn Marie Croxford, you are the love of my life. This book is merely a reflection of the FIRE I feel for you. Thank you for loving me unconditionally and supporting me as I wrote this book. You have given me a higher purpose for all that I do. You make me a better man. I thank God every day that we met. I am so glad I waited for you. You were worth the wait and I am FIRED UP every day we are together!

Kerrie Lundahl, thanks for being such a great friend to JeniLynn! I owe you for life!

Emma, my precious princess, thanks for teaching me what it means to be FIRED UP!

To the Croxford family—Sherri, Jason, JuliAnn, Jessica, JamiSue, and James—you are all AWESOME! I am so blessed be in your lives.

Mark Deleon (aka Maverick), my mentor, thank you for calling in sick to work, seeing me on television, writing down my website, and hiring me to speak to your Texas Teen Ambassadors. You changed my life forever. Our friendship and your mentorship have given me a life I only dreamed of. Keep making a difference in all the lives you touch.

E. Don Brown, thank you for believing in me and giving me an opportunity. You are such a great mentor and father figure and friend. Your wisdom and passion for kids inspires me to want to do even more.

Introduction

What does it mean to be FIRED UP? It means to be on FIRE for life—FIRED UP for what you "get to do," and for "why" you do what you do.

The late great Philadelphia Flyer Hockey Coach, Fred Shero, famously said to his players, "Success is not the result of spontaneous combustion. You must first set yourself on fire!" I really believe that Shero is right. Many of us are not burned out—we are just not FIRED UP!

There are countless books, audio programs, and seminars out there all about finding your passion, and being happy and successful. Most are great and many can work for you. My own bookshelf is full of books—each of which I hoped would be *the one* to change my life. Each title felt like it had the answer to solve my problem at the moment. I would read bits and pieces and mine what I needed from each. I even subscribed to the motivational leaflet called *Bits and Pieces,* which offered short inspirational stories and quotes that made me feel good.

Don't Let Your Life's Desires Collect Dust

I would buy books that I leafed through in the bookstore only to have them collect dust on my nightstand—haven't we all done this? I would carry these books around with me, hoping that the words would leap from the pages into my psyche and change my emotional wellbeing. But they were all missing that special something that could really inspire me—something that could really make me feel FIRED UP to get out there and do something wonderful with the precious life I was living.

There are three key books I have read cover to cover that have changed my life and state of mind. *Return to Love* by Marianne Williamson, *The Untethered Soul: The Journey Beyond Yourself* by Michael A. Singer, and *WE: Understanding the Psychology of Romantic Love* by Robert A. Johnson. I carry the first two wherever I go and do my best never to forget what I learned in the third.

This book, *FIRED UP!*, is my personal philosophy, my very own seven-step strategy for tapping into your own inner joy, success, motivation, and most of all, happiness. My hope is that *FIRED UP!* will be the kind of book that you can refer to time and again to help transform how you feel and think. I want the *aha!* moments to flow from the pages into your brain and help you shift your attitude to one of joy and happiness, while inspiring you to take action immediately on your goals and dreams. I hope that you will refer to or quote this book when helping your friends through challenges or talking to your kids about how to live life. It is my hope that you will one day say, "This book changed my life!" I want you to tell your friends about what you learned and hopefully say, "You have to read this book!" Or better yet, "This book inspired me so much, I bought a copy for you as a gift!"

Wandering Outside Your Comfort Zone Can Be Tough
What I am describing here includes my hopes and dreams for you. Obviously, I do not have control over you or what will happen if you read this book. I have come to realize that many people really fear change. However, having said this, I also believe most people *feel a deep desire* to change; they just don't know how to go about it or perhaps may be too afraid of the unknown. Many of us want to talk about changing, think about changing, and dream about a life that is different than the one we are currently living. We want to rewrite our history. But rewriting history and creating real change takes time, work, and courage. And it's often uncomfortable. Change can be hard; change can be scary. Change often requires stepping into the great wide unknown.

Wandering out of your comfort zone can be tough and quite difficult even in the best of circumstances.

I'll use myself as an example. I'm not a natural-born writer. Words only come to me with difficulty after hours of staring at a blank page. I have a ridiculously tight deadline for this book, and I procrastinated for the first two days! I am thinking to myself, *I am not sure if I can even pull it off.* It isn't fun for me being cooped up in a hotel room while life is happening all around me. Right now, I am speaking at the Ultimate Life Summit in Orlando, Florida, near Disney World. As I write this book, all I really want to do is get out there and talk, play, and laugh! But let's assume I didn't, because here you hold the finished product.

Instead, I realized that I needed to rethink my procrastination and negative and doubtful approach in order to get this book done—a scary endeavor!

I really had to look inward in order to get started. Why am I writing this book? Questioning "why" I do something is what motivates me most—and doing so leads me then to ask "what." What FUELS my fire to write this book? What really gets my motor running? Well, it comes back to accountability to myself. I want to write this book for me! I want to measure up and live my greater purpose. I have always believed I could write a book. I just never really tried before. I have something worthwhile to say and I want to put it out there. So here it goes.

Getting Fired Up Requires Evolution

I also have a greater purpose. I want to write this book to help others. I love FIRING UP my audiences. But then I go home. And so do they. The spoken word is powerful. But it is fleeting. I want to remind people about what I said and inspire everyone to take the actions I facilitate in my presentations. I want to give people the same tools and strategies I use and get them FIRED UP for life! This book is a dream come true and helps me fulfill my life mission. In addition, I want to be a part of the evolution of the species. I realize that when I change and grow, and when you change and grow, the whole world changes for the better.

I love the life I have today because of the things I have done with the help of my mentors, counselors, life coaches, friends, family, other speakers, and authors. Sharing their wisdom and the steps they continue to pass on to me is a display of my appreciation to them and my way of paying it forward.

Write What You Feel to the Love of Your Life

Recently, the love of my life told me to write this book to her. It got me FIRED UP just thinking of us, our love, our family, what we have, how we met, and our life together. If I didn't write and practice these Seven Steps in my FIRED UP acronym, then I would not have met her. That had me thinking that others might need these tools, too. Everyone deserves this gift. I want this book to inspire others to get FIRED UP and follow this lead. I *have* to write this book. I have gauged that the audiences I speak to want more than I can provide in just the few short hours I speak to them. So here are the strategies that have changed my life forever. They have set me free. Now, do you think that I am too lazy to get this book project done and published on deadline? No way! Why? Because I am FIRED UP!

Inventory Your Life—You Will Be Glad You Did

I am taking INVENTORY of what I have. I have 120 hours to write this book. That is 7,200 minutes! Okay, here's the mind shift: I have tons of time! I also have lots of love and support. I say to myself: I *am* a talented writer and speaker and I have a real gift for connecting people. I want to share this gift with others. Great musicians are compelled to play music, great athletes feel they must play ball, and great leaders are driven to lead. I want to share my enthusiasm. Therefore, I must write; I want to share my inspiration. I will shout it from the rooftops and I am driven to put it in print for all of those who want to get up and get going with their lives. I will do it for all those people who I will never meet. This book must be written! Another minute wasted is blasphemy! Oh, and I do my best work under pressure. How about you? We all work differently and have different levels of energy and capacity to make great things happen. INVENTORY what drives you to the end zone and beyond!

Escape Shame and Reframe the Way You Look at Life

So, next, I start working hard on REFRAMING my attitude. I think a little more about everything I am writing here in this introduction. I keep telling myself, I *know* I can do this! I say to myself, I *am* a great writer and I want to share my inspiration with everybody. This *is* going to be fun! In five days, the majority of the work will be done. The editors will polish it and make it all flow. I love writing. By putting the strategies of my speech into print, I *can* help countless others! I am excited to be an author. How cool does that sound: Aric Bostick, renowned speaker, best-selling author, and television star? (That last one is my next big dream! More on that later.) WOO-HOO! I *can* do this! WOW! See how it works? Try it.

Get Energized and Declare Your Mission

I am starting to feel the critical ENERGY required to write this book. I can keep the flow of energy rising! It is 12:32 a.m. as I write this. I speak tomorrow to 150 students from around the world at the Ultimate Life Summit. I can't wait to share my journey and triumph with them. Talk about living your message! I think I should shower, or eat something, or go for a run, or just go to sleep and start tomorrow. But then I think, how many times have I said that? I'll start tomorrow. I'll exercise tomorrow. I'll call about that opportunity tomorrow. I'll ask for help tomorrow. I'll end that relationship that is killing me tomorrow. I'll clean that closet tomorrow. No, I think, I must write this book—now! I will finish this introduction *tonight*. I have just refueled with some fruit and water and a two-hour power nap. One week of minimal sleep won't kill me. I am going to be fine for tomorrow! I must DECLARE it now—this book *will be finished in five days*! This is my mission. I will get this done! It's my declaration. What's yours?

Understand the Power of Touching Others—This Book Is for You
I UNDERSTAND who this book is for. It isn't just about me. It is about all the people who will be served after they take this book back to their work teams or family. It is for all of the people who don't believe that they can go on living a certain way. It's for all of you who want to change. You feel you have to change. You are FIRED UP! This book is for the cynical employee who thinks that his job doesn't make a difference and everyone else is to blame for why he is unhappy or why the company stinks. It's for the human resource manager who knows she can make a difference but has her life sucked out of her by the Negative Nancys she might have to endure each day.

Difficulties Can Be Good
This book is for the teacher who has not seen a pay raise in years; has had his or her pension cut and benefits reduced; has no job security; has little support from parents, bosses, and coworkers; and is expected to change lives and inspire students to want to learn, but with limited resources. It's for the teenager who was abused, the student with a learning disability, the single mom trying to learn a second language so that she can get a job and support her family to give them a better quality of life. It's for all of us who have suffered with anxiety or insecurity about not measuring up or being enough in some unique way. We messed up at work, lost an important file, had a fight with our partner, we are the black sheep of the family, we don't trust ourselves because of the mistakes we have made. Life is difficult. But difficulties can be good—showing us what we are made of and strengthening our character and our determination.

But many people have really tough and unimaginable challenges. Sixty-nine days in a mine—that is difficult; 127 hours trapped under a boulder—that is truly difficult. Losing a limb, a child, a parent, a best friend—that is unimaginably difficult. Fighting cancer, going through a divorce, finding out your best friend betrayed you—that is difficult. Being abused in some way—any way—by someone you trusted—that is difficult. I have experienced difficult. So have you. Somehow, most of us have handled it. I know that I can handle it and I believe you can, too. Five days to write a book for the greater good of people who, just like me, have suffered and want to get over it? Yeah, I get it. I have to write this book!

Purpose Behind the Passion
All we have to do is be fully PRESENT. We need to live in the moment. Keep a good attitude and remember your purpose and passion—like I am remembering my purpose and passion behind writing this book. What keeps me centered? One thing I do is Bikram yoga—that's yoga in a 106-degree room for 90 minutes. My yogi tells me just to breathe in and out and focus on that breath. I do, and I forget about the heat. I slow down, I get present, and all of a sudden my fears and anxieties vanish. So now, I must be present and breathe, and then this writing will get done and with greater ease. I tell myself, this is no big deal. I concentrate on just being in this moment and enjoying the process. I focus and think about who I am writing for and I stay in the moment. This will be a gift to so many if I just stay in the present moment and write from the heart and share my experience. I feel a peace wash over me. I am FIRED UP!

And that is how it works. It is that simple and sometimes that challenging. It is now 2:25 a.m. I still have to get up in five hours. But now I am inspired! I am FIRED UP!

Fired Up for Success!

There you have it. This is my personal and powerful process for getting FIRED UP! In the next seven chapters, I will share more experiences with you and give you tips, tools, and techniques that you, too, can use to get FIRED UP every day. I will be clear and concise: Do THIS and YOU WILL GET THAT! But *you* have to do it! This book will not change your life! It will be up to you to do the work and create the life you want. So decide now if this is going to be another book on your shelf collecting dust, or the beginning steps to taking action toward who you want to be. On the other side of this amazing process is the real you who you have always imagined.

One final thought. Fred Shero also said, "When you have bacon and eggs for breakfast, the chicken makes a contribution, but the pig makes a commitment."

DECIDE TODAY!

COMMIT NOW!

GET FIRED UP!

—Aric Bostick
September 2012

Chapter 1

FUEL: What Fuels Your Tank?

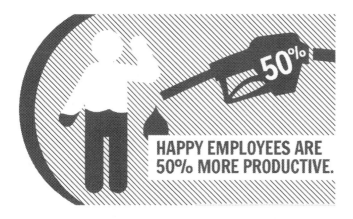

HAPPY EMPLOYEES ARE 50% MORE PRODUCTIVE.

The first step to getting FIRED UP is to figure out precisely what FIRES YOU UP! This can be challenging at times because we lose focus about what we want and how to get it.

I meet so many different people who are simply unclear about what they want. I believe when we solely focus on what we think we WANT, NEED, OR DESIRE, we will come up short every time. How many times have you received the raise, earned the recognition, bought the new car, or gained the relationship and you were still unhappy and feeling empty? My experience is that our fuel does not come from an outside source or material thing—it comes from the very core of our being. If you want to find out what fuels you, you have to think outside of what you want for *you*.

You Can't Always Get What You Want but If You *Give*, You'll Get What You Need

What exactly do you want to give or contribute and why? When you figure this out, you'll begin to get excited, your creative energy will begin to flow, and you won't always be thinking about the outcome or some bottom line quota you are trying to meet. You will become on FIRE because of what you are going to GIVE, not because of what you are going to GET. The interesting thing is that when you start giving, you most certainly will start receiving, but that part won't matter as much to you. Your shift in focus is the beginning of your new change and growth! And that results in self-fulfillment! You may not get precisely what you *think* you want immediately, but something good will come eventually. You won't have that feeling of falling short because you'll have satisfaction from within yourself—a reward to yourself, in a sense.

Every wonderful thing in my life has come about from the question, "How can I serve?" Zig Ziglar told his readers, "You can get everything in life you want if you help enough other people get what they want." I think that's one powerful statement. I became a high school teacher and coach because I had a coach who made a difference in my life and I wanted to do the same for other young people. One of my students asked me to give a motivational speech at his church one Sunday evening. That church told another church and then another and before I knew it, I was being paid to speak on a regular basis. I got to do something I loved, something that served others, and something I happily would do for free—but being paid made it that much sweeter! I stumbled into this amazing new career and it was the end result of something *I never even knew I wanted*—I was riding the wave of inner fulfillment.

The New Sustainable Energy

You may be thinking to yourself, "What does this have to do with me being FIRED UP for my life, my job, my organization, my community, or my bottom line?" You may be trying to get your managers to be better leaders of your stores. You might be trying to increase your sales. You may want your students to pay attention in class and perform well on their standardized tests. You may want your employees to show up on time and perform their jobs with a good attitude.

The point is this: What fuels your fire is *WHAT you decide to give, WHY it's important for you to give it,* and *WHO you decide to be because of it*!

When you think of what you can give, then everything changes. When you change your thinking from being needy to believing you have something worthwhile to offer, people will be attracted to what you have to give. People will want to buy your products and your managers will be fired up to lead their teams because of all you give to them. Sales will increase because of your phenomenal service and all that you stand for. Your students will be so excited to listen to your lessons, turn their work in, and give you their best because you are giving your best instruction—and doing so from a thoughtful and inspired position. People will follow your lead because you will be leading with a bigger purpose. People will know when you are fired up because your passion and energy will become a raging WILD FIRE! Bruce Springsteen sang it best: "You can't start a fire without a spark!" *You* are the spark.

Wikipedia says that "the positive effects of fire include *stimulating growth* and maintaining various ecological systems. Fire has been used by humans for cooking, generating heat, signaling, and *propulsion purposes.*" Fire is part of the evolution of the species and it will take hold of you if you start it! You can't help but to spread it to all those you touch! So my message is this: If you want to change your company, or your schools, or the lives around you, then start by *changing yourself.* Find out what you want to give that could start a fire of enthusiasm and passion to stimulate growth in your world and propel you toward what you really, really want! When you are whole and complete, you have so much to offer. Your company, too, has so much to offer, as does your organization, your school, your students, and your colleagues. How can you better serve those you work with and for?

Your Gift to the World Is to Serve

The philosophy of service fuels the biggest and most successful companies and people in the world. Simon Sinek outlines in his powerful book, *Start with Why: How Great Leaders Inspire Everyone to Take Action,* how Apple and Southwest Airlines revolutionized their markets due to their desire to serve the greater good. Apple wanted to level the business playing field by making computers that were affordable and easy to use by everybody. Southwest Airlines wanted to make travel affordable for everyone. These are now two of the most profitable companies in their industries. These companies don't just make computers or fly airplanes. They FIRE US UP! *That is their gift!* People who love Apple products are so passionate about them that they're willing to camp outside for days—on sidewalks!—to be the first ones to get anything new from Apple. If you have ever been on a Southwest Airlines flight, you know the flight attendants are ON FIRE! They serve you with a smile, they joke over the intercom, they make flying fun, and they inspire me to want to fly more.

Now it is your turn, your life, and your world. What do you want to give to the world? Let me be clear. I am not saying that you should not want any compensation or fair exchange for your values and services. I don't want you to live in a shack and be a martyr any more than I want to be a motivational speaker living in a van down by the river (as Chris Farley's *Saturday Night Live* character Matt Foley used to say in one of his famous skits).

Apple and Southwest Airlines are billion dollar companies. They serve the world, create innovations and services that serve us all, and are abundant and prosperous. What I am clearly stating is this: What gifts do you want to give the world? Why is using those gifts important to you?

Again, I'll use myself as an example: My fire is fueled by motivating and inspiring people through my speaking career and daily living. I want to help set people free from the chains of being less than the best version of who they are—and inspire them to do what they love and share their gifts with others through whatever it is that they are doing. I want to FIRE UP people to be the absolute best they can be! Are you unhappy with your current situation? Then change your mind-set to being the consummate best at whatever you do, to giving as much as you possibly can—whether you are a janitor or a CEO or a student. Put your best foot forward in all your efforts and wear a smile like a uniform!

Why is this so important to me and why am I sharing this with you? I really enjoy and treasure my life today. I want you to enjoy and treasure your life, too! I want to share the tools in this book for living FIRED UP, and explain the principle behind the message. That's my gift to you.

Now what is your gift to the world?

FIRED UP and Doing Something About It! Step #1

1. What is your gift to the world? List your gifts and all that you want to do with them.

_____

_____

_____

2. Why should you give this gift to all those you would give it to?

_____

_____

_____

3. Who and what would be served by your gift?

_____

_____

_____

Chapter 2

INVENTORY: Take Stock of Your Life

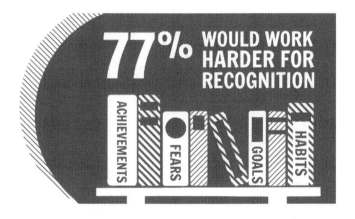

WOO-HOO! Outstanding job! Now that you know what FUELS YOU, let's figure out what is holding you back! For me, FEAR and RESENTMENT were the number one blocks in my life. I used to fear failure, rejection, and losing money. I would play out the scene in my head of all the negative things that could happen or what I would feel if these things happened. But then I started to imagine the consequences if I did not try to fulfill my dreams and goals. What if I never tried to become a full-time speaker? What if I didn't get over this fear of rejection and ask for a date? What if I never overcame this need for constant love and approval? The list could go on forever.

Look in the Mirror

Being human can be tough. There are reasons why many people overeat, abuse alcohol and drugs, stay in toxic relationships, work insane hours, watch hours of television or movies, or spend countless hours procrastinating. The reason is often the *fear of change*. It is difficult and scary to take a hard look at your life and realize you don't like what you see. It is easier to distract yourself with destructive behaviors and not face what is keeping you from being the best version of you. Many people either play it too safe or throw caution to the wind. How do we create the life we want and achieve our goals personally, professionally, physically, relationally, and beyond? I believe it's by facing our fears and resentments and ridding ourselves of the harmful and malignant thoughts that cloud our thinking and hold us back.

It's my experience that the solution to our problems always lies within us. We know we need to make changes, but we may be just too scared to do it. I believe everyone fears change at some level. We make excuses for ourselves or maybe deep down inside we secretly enjoy the drama. We don't even know what it would be like to live without carrying that security blanket of fear or resentment—those feelings are oftentimes so deeply ingrained in us.

Ditch the What Ifs

I've spent my entire life figuring out how to be happy. I call it the "I'll be happy when…" syndrome: I'll be happy when I get the promotion, get the raise, get recognized for my efforts, get into a relationship, get out of a relationship, and the list goes on. My "I'll be happy when…" list has looked something like this: I will be happy when Mom is happy, when Dad is proud of me, when my brother and I get along, when I stop getting picked on, when I am sixteen years old and can drive, when I graduate from high school and go to college, when I finish college, when I pay off my debt, when I get the right job, when my peers respect me, when I receive love and approval, when my talent is recognized, when I become a full-time speaker and get paid to travel and speak, when I find the perfect mate who fits all of my criteria, when I get married, when I have kids, and on and on!

I don't know what's on your list. But I do know we all have fears, worries, resentments, and thoughts that hold us back. The good news is that's all they are—*thoughts*. You are not the embodiment of your fears, resentments, neurotic thoughts, or what you do or don't have. These are just thoughts to which we often give too much power.

Many of our wants and desires are actually based on lack of something and certain deficiencies we are experiencing. We let the *what ifs* shackle us to inaction: What if I only had better parents? What if I hadn't made that decision? What if I'd gone to college? What if that person didn't leave? What if I didn't get that disease? Maybe then I could be happy and all my problems would be solved. We think our past has damaged and scarred us in such a way that we can't move forward and enjoy our jobs, lives, and relationships. Change runs the risk of physical and mental challenges, failure, and possibly getting hurt. I don't know many people who openly embrace getting hurt. Do you?

Letting Go Sets You Free

I don't think I'm oversimplifying when I offer three words for handling the reasons why you are burned out, stressed out, and fearful: **LET IT GO!**

By letting go, you give yourself permission to stop wasting your precious energy on what hasn't been working for you. Why let these things keep us from success in the workplace, at home, and with our family and friends? LET IT GO now and GET FIRED UP!

How do we begin to make positive change? First, by letting go of those insecurities we hold dear. Then, by taking INVENTORY of our strengths. Are you FIRED UP and ready to DO SOMETHING ABOUT IT? Then keep reading...

FIRED UP and Doing Something About It! Step #2

1. Make a list of all your strengths on the lines below. This might be
   difficult at first. Enlist a friend to remind you of the value that others
   see in you. What makes you feel great about you? What are you
   good at? What do you love to do with passion? What would you do
   seven days a week even if you weren't being paid to do it?

   _____

   _____

   _____

2. What would you like to change about yourself? What fears,
   resentments, or habits have to go NOW so you can feel good about
   yourself? How will you face down your fears? How will you confront
   and recognize the things that hold you back and make you less than
   your best? How will you grow your greater potential?

   _____

   _____

   _____

3. Circle YES or NO—Are you ready to let this go today?

   Sign here, committing to begin this critical process:

   _____

   Signature:
   Date:

   Congratulations! Picture me giving you a big HIGH-FIVE! You are
on your way and I look forward to being a part of your journey as you
read on in Chapter 3.

Chapter 3

REFRAME: Shift Your Perspective

EMPLOYEE RECOGNITION CAN BOOST PERFORMANCE 44%

Whew! Don't you feel lighter? You have taken inventory of all your strengths. You've become more aware that you have many gifts to offer. Hopefully, you are now feeling freer from the chains of fear, resentment, and pain that have been holding you back. I am fully aware that letting go is a process. Your fears and resentments may sneak up on you again. I encourage you to keep letting them go. Keep journaling, going to counseling, or talking to friends—but no matter what, don't let fear and resentment stop you from moving forward.

The Wisdom of Bob Newhart

So how do we create this new mental habit? How does a person stop smoking, stop drinking, stop running into the corner of the coffee table?

We just STOP IT! There is a great *MAD TV* skit where famous TV icon Bob Newhart plays a therapist and Mo Collins plays a patient who fears being buried alive in a box. She shares how this fear is ruining her life. The therapist tells her, "I am going to tell you two words that I want you to take out of this office and incorporate into your life: STOP IT!"

The patient replies, "So what are you saying?" She continues, "I have had this fear since childhood!" The therapist interrupts her and says, "No, no! We don't go there! Just STOP IT!"

She shares other issues with him, and his constant advice is just simply to say, "STOP IT!" Sometimes we hate when the answer is that simple, *but it is*. Whatever you are doing now that is not working to better you, simply STOP IT!

Adopting Your New Attitude

Now, what do we do with this newfound free space? We replace it with a NEW PERSPECTIVE, a new thought, a forever changed attitude! I have used this concept in every area of my life. For example, without the difficulties I faced in childhood, I wouldn't have learned how to change and grow as a person at such a young age. My journey toward self-discovery started early because if I didn't start it, who knows where I might have ended up. You're on a journey, too! My father's recovery from alcoholism was an inspiration and led him to become dedicated to personal growth. He would take me with him to motivational seminars and workshops and share his books with me. I was reading Zig Ziglar's *See You at the Top* as a freshman in high school! And look where I am today. I get to share what I learned and have successfully implemented into my life with people from around the world.

The Tough Situation You Live in Doesn't Have to Live in You

Everything that happened *to* me has happened *for* me. Having experienced the awkward teenage years with divorced parents, a blended family, acne, braces, and countless other challenges helped me to understand the people to whom I speak and what they are up against. I can love them unconditionally and give them encouragement and hope that the hardships of their life will pass. I wouldn't change a thing from my past now. There's a quote I often use in my presentations: "The tough situation you live in doesn't have to live in you!"

You can REFRAME whatever situation you live in. As a motivational speaker, I often have to reframe my perspective. Most people see the happy, FIRED UP me on stage. But they have no idea I've endured airport parking and security, plane delays, lost luggage, and long walks to rental cars in rain, snow, and heat just to get there. Then there's finding the hotel, finding the location of the event, racing from the event back to the airport to catch yet another plane to do it all over again.

But I will never complain about it. NOT ANYMORE! My new perspective is, "I don't have to speak all over the world; I get to!" I used to complain about all my frequent travel and how I couldn't meet anyone because I was always gone. If not for an eight-day road trip and jumping on the right Hertz rental car bus, I would have never met the love of my life. I would never have met all the amazing students, educators, parents, and fired up employees I call friends today. I see how much fun I can have at all the different places I go. I have a friend in the industry who says, "I love traveling and I haven't bought shampoo or lotion in years!" I now tell people, "I have the privilege of seeing the country and getting paid to do it and I have a never ending supply of little peanut snacks!" I think about how I would have never gone to Crawford, Nebraska. But I am glad and thankful I did. The person who hired me there became my best friend in the world.

Do You Want to Be Happy?

Every job has its good points and its not-so-good points. So does every family, friend, coworker, exercise routine, diet, city, and state. But when we can change our perspective and reframe it, *we take control of how we view the world* and life gets a whole lot better really fast. As I said earlier,

I am currently speaking at the Ultimate Life Summit in Orlando, Florida. I am staying at a five-star resort and I get to go to Disney World every day. One of the attendees is from Colombia, South America, and I heard him tell another attendee how much he is enjoying having reliable running water this week.

Running water as a luxury? That changed my perspective in a hurry! The more mind-blowing thing is that he loves his country with an intensity I have never seen here in America. When I'm on stage and ask, "Where are my Colombians?" they cheer and dance like they won the lottery. They have no running water in parts of their country and they are cheering for how proud they are to be from there! They love what they have and appreciate what they don't have. How's that for a positive outlook on life?

My favorite book, *The Untethered Soul,* which I mentioned earlier, is written by Michael A. Singer, and has a chapter titled "The Path to Unconditional Happiness." Singer says that you really only have one choice in life: "Do you want to be happy or do you not want to be happy? It's that simple. Once you make that choice, your path through life becomes totally clear."

So do you want to be happy or not? Take a moment to REFRAME your life and your current situation and see how much better you feel. How much better could your life be if you chose to REFRAME things and adopt a new and healthier perspective, filled with greater appreciation and gratitude? My guess is that you would truly be FIRED UP!

Fired Up and Doing Something About It! Step #3

1. What are ways you can begin to see life differently? Individually REFRAME your career, relationships, motherhood, fatherhood, health, hobbies, interests you haven't pursued yet but want to try, and so on. Build a new framework for every part of your life, then get ready to display it to others in your gallery of life.

2. List three of your major accomplishments. Make these things that you are particularly proud of. You may have finished a marathon, but come in last. So what? You finished! That's an accomplishment. Reflect on your personal and professional life, community service, recent events, or events from years past. Write about those experiences that fired you up here. Re-live what you do so well.

_____

_____

_____

Bonus tip: Instead of thinking about all the "to-do" lists in your daily life, why not start making "accomplishment lists"? They take the burden of more to do off your shoulders and start lightening your load of responsibility with a sense of appreciation for how amazing you can be when put to the test.

3. Focus on and list three things, or more, that you LOVE about your life! Remember, the mundane can be powerful. That first cup of coffee on the porch each morning can be something to which you love treating yourself. Watching your child sleep may give you great inner peace. People-watching at the airport can bring a smile to your face when you're stressed and hungry. Helping an elderly person who's struggling to get into a doorway at the doctor's office can make you feel like life's greatest hero. What you love about your life doesn't have to be huge, or about winning, or about flashy possessions.

_____

_____

_____

Chapter 4

ENERGIZE: Exercise, Get R&R, Eat Well

NEW ATTITUDES breed new energy! Have you ever looked at something differently and had the new perspective re-energize you? Our attitudes affect our energy! The question then becomes how do we keep our energy flowing on a daily basis? It also turns out that what we put into our bodies affects our attitudes and energy as well. It is very simple. To stay FIRED UP we have to put good fuel in our tanks. I believe we have to think of our bodies like vehicles. We would not fill our cars with sugar. But we do it to ourselves every day. And we use loads of it! A recent United Press International article[1] reports that the

---

1 UPI.com, "Americans Eat 22 Teaspoons of Sugar a Day," *Health News,* April 30, 2011, http://www.upi.com/Health_News/2011/04/30/Americans-eat-22-teaspoons-of-sugar-a-day/UPI-35521304221808/.

average American consumes 22.2 teaspoons—about 355 calories—of sugar daily. I am not saying we shouldn't ever have a cookie. But when we overdo it, we'll feel pretty crummy after the ups and downs of that sugar roller coaster.

Nothing Tastes as Good as Healthy Feels

It is also recommended that we get the oil in our cars changed every 3,000 to 4,000 miles. Are you the type to wait until the check engine light comes on, or do you wait until smoke rises from under the hood of your car? It's awfully embarrassing to explain to the mechanic why you blew up your engine. Now instead of a $50 oil change, you are looking at replacing a $5,000 engine. We all know if we take care of ourselves each day, we won't break down and need an overhaul later. Have you ever waited until dinner to eat something and when you finally did, you ate everything in sight? I am not a nutritionist. I was raised by a Southern cook who fed me fried food and the best desserts imaginable. I didn't eat my first salad until I was 25 years old and my first regular intake of fruit was shortly after that. It has been an evolution for me to learn to eat to live rather than live to eat. I know now that nothing tastes as good as healthy feels.

Garbage In, Garbage Out

What you put in your body matters. There's endless research that shows a balanced diet rich in fruits, vegetables, whole grains, and limited amounts of lean meats will help you keep your motor running for a longer time. I want to live a long time and I hope you do, too. I won't tell you what to eat or drink, but you know deep down inside that if you are sucking down sodas, eating junk food all day, and overdoing the alcohol, chances are you won't feel good. Did you know our bodies often disguise thirst for hunger? Drink as much water as you can. Water is the key to life and so good for your blood flow, skin, and energy. Stay hydrated and you will feel great!

Remember in Chapter 1 when I asked you to write about all the gifts you have to offer the world and your big reason WHY you want to share those gifts with others? We can't share our gifts if we are unhealthy or worse yet—no longer here. My dad jokes that he wants to die healthy! Nobody makes it out of this world alive. But there is no reason to suffer from poor health because you did not take care of yourself. Being unhealthy is often a choice—maybe not a conscious one, but a choice nonetheless. More importantly, we can't share our gifts and talents fully if we are operating with an empty tank. We certainly cannot state that we truly are FIRED UP if we are running on fumes.

Choose Health, Choose Abundance, Choose Peace of Mind

I am pretty adamant about this because I am living proof that good nutrition and regular exercise can transform your life. We must choose abundance and peace of mind if we want to have them in our lives. How we get there is something we figure out along the way. When I sought the help of a nutritionist and a physical trainer, and started doing Bikram yoga, my life and energy to live it changed for the better. I also started reading and watching movies about health and what is in our foods, and learned strategies for eating healthier at home and on the road. I simply started eating to live longer and feel good. I also noticed that when I eat and keep my health in mind, my moods stabilized, I felt more at peace, I needed less sleep, and I felt happier, more spontaneous, and more fun. The pleasant after effect was also that my waistline and stomach trimmed down! Everything about my life got better when I started putting foods in my body that supported my energy throughout the day.

Get Up, Get Going, Get Energized for Life!

We must move our bodies to generate energy. When a car sits unused for too long, often it won't crank up. We may hear it try, but it just won't move. We have to drive it to keep the engine running regularly.

The same goes with aircraft and boats. Therefore, the same goes for our bodies. We have to move our bodies! If you are serious about getting FIRED UP then FIRE UP your body and take it for a spin! Go for a walk, take a bike ride, run, do yoga, try Zumba classes, take up kick boxing, go to spin class, lift weights with a friend, or just walk around the block after dinner.

Your body is a magnificent machine. Make it work for you! Exercise for just ten minutes and watch how much better you feel. Research shows that if you exercise ten minutes three times a day, it will give you the same benefit of exercising thirty minutes straight. Can you schedule ten minutes a day? How about thirty minutes? How about an hour? The next time you are on the couch feeling exhausted, get up and put on your workout clothes. Then go back and lie on the couch. See how quickly you get up and exercise. When you act enthusiastic, you will become enthusiastic! Automatically. You'll soon feel the urge and the surge.

Go to the gym and sit in the parking lot, or just walk in the gym and look around. Chances are that in both cases you will find yourself feeling the urge just to get started. Half the challenge is just getting dressed to get going. So look like you are going to work out, and watch how the feelings and actions will follow.

Get a Life—Relax and Unplug

Finally, rest, relax, and have some fun! Get a life! What is your next big thing? What are you up to? If your answer is the same old thing, you need to change that. It is recommended that people get seven to eight hours of sleep each night. I personally advocate also taking short power naps when you get the opportunity. Even ten minutes of snooze time can ignite your enthusiasm. These practices are part of my energy maintenance plan. So schedule in your chill time just to sit back and unwind.

But I also want you to consider the ideas of RECHARGING and REDEDICATING yourself. What would recharge your battery? Do something that lifts you up spiritually, plugs you in mentally, and gets you going physically! Have you ever wanted to learn how to play the guitar? Learn French? Take ballroom dancing lessons? Master a new software program on your computer? What could you dedicate yourself to that would really get you excited? It's like putting new spark plugs in your engine. You will have a new fire within and you will look forward to getting off work to go do this activity. It will also energize you at work because you will be up to something new. Your life is more than just work now. You won't be burned out; you will be FIRED UP!

Consider how much time you have spent relaxing by watching television. Did you feel better afterward? Maybe, but other times you may have felt worse. According to the A.C. Nielsen Co., the average American watches four hours of television a day. That is twenty-eight hours a week, which translates into two months of non-stop television viewing! I have been that person! How about you? When I limited my viewing time, I got so much more done. But here's what's more important: I spend more time with my family and friends. I enjoy relating to others and being a part of the world more than I did watching it go by on a TV screen.

Go on a Media/Techno Strike!
Do you ever unplug during the day? I'm talking about turning off your iPod, iPad, iPhone, and any other electronic devices you use regularly. Go on a media/technology strike for an hour or two and see how you spend your time. Maybe you can cook a nutritious meal for your family and eat it with them, minus the distractions! The constant interruptions of pings and beeps can really derail your train of thought when you're trying to chill out and spend quality time with those you love and care about most. My friend Diana Damron calls cell phones "triangular bullies." Are you being bullied by your cell phone or other electronic device? If yes, put a stop to the bullying now.

Do Something for the First Time Again

Finally, rededicate yourself to something you've always loved and enjoyed, but have stopped doing because you won't make the time. Play the piano, play a round of golf, plant a garden, meet your best friend for lunch, or take your child to the park. What activities did you enjoy in the past that you may have abandoned over the years? Rededicate yourself to doing these things again. One of my favorite quotes is, "When is the last time you did something for the first time?" RECHARGE by starting something new. Do something for the first time, or REDEDICATE yourself to doing something you used to do, but now enjoy it as if it was the first time all over again!

Let's make a plan now for you to ENERGIZE yourself and get your candle burning bright again for years to come!

FIRED UP and Doing Something About It! Step #4

1. Avoid the energy sucks! This requires making a list of what you might be doing as a habit—things that suck the energy out of you and actually break down your body and make you feel bad about yourself. Then, channel your inner Bob Newhart therapist and STOP IT!

_____

_____

_____

2. Replace that old bad habit with a new good one. Create a list of what types of exercise and nutritional habits you can adopt that will support your long-term health and wellness. List the resources, including people who can coach you in the moment. I guarantee that this will help you with your plan of action and support you in your new life goals.

_____

_____

_____

3. Declare a call to action now! Create a plan to recharge and rededicate yourself to things you have always wanted to try—or those things that you used to enjoy. Check the Internet for activities and events in your area. Next, think ahead. What can you experiment with and try that you have never tried before? Skydiving? Skateboarding? Writing the great American novel? Building a house? The sky's the limit. Shoot for the moon and even if you miss, you'll likely land among the stars.

_____

_____

_____

Chapter 5

DECLARE: What's Your Mission?

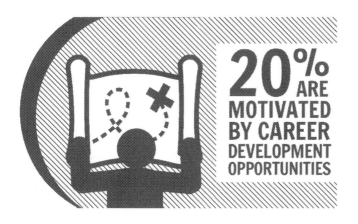

Now that we are fueled up, have taken inventory, have reframed our perspective, and have become energized, it is time to DECLARE and DECIDE what we will do and who we will become from this point forward. The power of our thoughts and words can literally move mountains—those enormous mountains of fear, disappointment, and lack of confidence that have been holding us back.

If You Declare It, It Will Come

The first real goal I ever set to paper was my desire to make the high school varsity basketball team as a sophomore. In the spring of my freshman year, our coach requested our goals for the next season. He asked, "What team do you WANT to make next season?" When someone asks what you want, that generally means you have a choice. I signed up for junior varsity to be on the same team as my friends. After writing our goals, we reviewed them with our coach one on one. It was in that meeting that Coach challenged me to try to make the varsity team. I knew of only one sophomore who had made varsity. His name was Brian and he worked harder than every one of us combined. He was determined to be the best player in our school and had a dream of playing college basketball. Coach believed I could achieve more and encouraged me to partner with Brian. I had to go for it!

I introduced myself to Brian and told him my goal. He graciously worked out with me. We invested our own time and money to attend summer basketball camps together. I really admired Brian. He had a burning desire to be the best he could be. He was not the fastest, the strongest, or the most graceful player on the team, but he was the best! All summer I followed his lead.

My skills improved but I still lacked confidence. I harbored doubts and feared failure, and at times it would really affect my game. My father had introduced me to the practice of affirmations a few years before, so I declared out loud every day, "I am a sophomore on the varsity basketball team!" I would say this hundreds of times a day, and really feel it to my core and in my bones. These affirmations began to sink into my subconscious. My confidence went up, and I played more like a guy on the varsity team. I made the varsity team as a sophomore that season. Ever since, I have been a goal setter and have declared what I want out loud.

Thoughts Become Things and the Truth Will Set You Free
We are what we routinely say, think, and do. Thoughts do become things. I believe declarations motivate us to do what we need to do to bring about truths in our lives. *Webster's New World College Dictionary* says that to declare something is to make it clearly known, state, or announce openly and formally, and to reveal one's true character or

identity. What do you declare? What is your truth about your life? What do you want to give, have, do, be, own, let go of, grow, or care for? Declare it! Make it specifically known what it is that you want! At Customs in the airport, we have to declare what goods we bring into a country when we travel. What are you going to bring into your life today? Well then, DECLARE IT!

What's on Your Five-Year Declaration List?
I own a book called *The 5 Book—Where Will You Be Five Years from Today?*

You can buy it at Live-Inspired.com. I bought it at La Costa Resort in Southern California, which is one of the pictures on my dream collage—my visual representation of my goals and dreams. A dream collage is a combination of visual images that give us a focal point to shoot for in life. If you dream about graduating with a doctorate from Columbia University, then you may have a photo on your collage board or poster that depicts a Columbia graduate student with arms outstretched, holding a diploma on graduation day. Or perhaps a photo of the campus is depicted on your poster board. Visualization is easier when we find visual examples of what we want and display them where we can absorb the ideas and attract the end results into our lives.

While at La Costa Resort, I was browsing the gift shop and came across a particular book. I had been procrastinating on some of my goals, like becoming an author, starring in my own TV show, and countless other personal and professional goals. The store had other tempting titles as well. I couldn't decide which one to get, so I asked the young lady behind the counter to help me decide, because I didn't have room in my crowded carry-on bag for four books. She said, "I would get *The 5 Book*!" I asked if she owned it. She said, "No, I have two toddlers and can't afford it." I replied, "Well, how about if I buy a copy for me and a copy for you and I will autograph yours and you autograph mine, and we will read it, work the steps, and see where we are in five years?" She was ecstatic and touched. We exchanged contact info and autographed each other's books.

Later that afternoon, I was trying to find something healthy for lunch, and my new friend said, "You should treat yourself to piece of chocolate cake! You are on vacation!" I replied, "In five years, I am going to be ripped. My five years started today!"

Your five years starts *the day you decide and DECLARE it*! Why not start today?

FIRED UP and Doing Something About It! Step #5

1. Visualize where you want to be in FIVE years and then describe your vision in detail.

    In five years, I will _____

    _____

    _____

    _____

2. Set a goal or two in the following areas, and feel free to add your own areas of focus. Be as specific as possible. At the end of each goal, write these words: "This or SOMETHING BETTER!"

    • Professional Goal: _____

    _____

    • Personal Goal: _____

    _____

    • Health Goal: _____

    _____

- Super Crazy Pie in the Sky Goal: _____

_____

3. Make an Action Plan. Write the specific steps you will take to turn these goals into accomplishments. When you do this, you breathe life into your plan. You give it depth and breadth. It's no longer just words on paper. It's experiential and alive.

- Professional Goal Action Plan: _____

_____

- Personal Goal Action Plan: _____

_____

- Health Goal Action Plan: _____

_____

- Super Crazy Pie in the Sky Goal Action Plan: _____

_____

4. Why NOT YOU? DECLARE it now! Now write a personalized list of 10 affirmations and declarations you want to hear come out of your mouth every day. For example: I deserve good things in life! I am so blessed! I am thankful for my good health! I am beautiful! I am worthy of receiving love! I can do this! I can lose weight! I will work out today! I will get healthy! I am grateful for my talents and abilities! I am so lucky! I am so fortunate! I have plenty of time! This is so much fun! I love being with you! What a great day I am having!

1. _____
2. _____
3. _____
4. _____
5. _____
6. _____
7. _____
8. _____
9. _____
10. _____

I want this to work for you! But only you can make it real. Make copies of your goals, declarations, and statements you desire to say all the time. Read them every morning, cut them up, put them on your wall at the office, on your bathroom mirror, and add them to your dream collage! The repetition of your affirmations draws them closer and closer to you, day after day.

Go the Extra Mile—Create a FIRED UP PORTRAIT OF YOUR FIRED UP LIFE!
Chunk down these areas and visualize your end results. What does it look like? What does it feel like? How does it smell? Where will you stand the day you achieve these results? What city will you be in? Who will be by your side? What will he or she represent to you?

Instructions: Look back at the goals you have written above and the steps you have taken in each of the previous chapters. Then make a list of all the things you want to see in your life and the things you want to let go of. Then go have some fun! Let's make a visual representation of your FIRED UP LIFE!

Go to Google Images and type in the words on your list. Copy and paste pictures of what your FIRED UP LIFE will look and feel like. You can also use magazines or your creative ability to draw your dreams. You can add your declarations and quotes to this portrait as well. There is no wrong way to create your FIRED UP LIFE!

Put your portrait in a prominent place so you can see it often and feel the feeling of dreams already being accomplished!

Dream it. See it. And then be it!

Chapter 6

UNDERSTAND: Step into Someone Else's Shoes

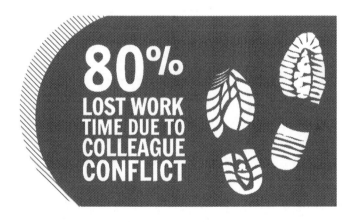

Tremendous job! You are ROCKING now! I am so impressed with your willingness to transform your life and take the initial steps toward being the person you truly are. So the question is, why do all of this? This is a lot of work. The reason goes back to having that FUEL for your fire. One reason you may be doing all of this is so that you can really serve and connect with others. Now that you have declared who you want to be and are working toward the best version of you, it is time to look beyond yourself and realize how much you really can affect others in a positive way. You can spread the fire and fan the flame in all those with whom you meet or work.

I have had times in my life when I was so focused on myself and my situation, my happiness, my career, my life, and what I was trying to accomplish, that I lost focus on the big picture. Now I know that my entire career and life really is based on giving. The happiness in my relationships is based on giving. My health and wellness is based on giving my body what it needs so I feel good, and can be my best and give my best to others. When I am happy, I can contribute to others' happiness. I meet so many student leaders, youth educators, sales people, managers, and leaders of organizations. The people who seem to be the happiest and are usually having the most fun and making the biggest difference are the people focused on consistently giving more to those they serve.

They do the little things, like greet people with a smile and learn people's names. They write thank you notes and learn about the personal lives of those they serve and those with whom they work.

Service with a Smile (and Cookies and Milk)

Early in my career as a speaker, I witnessed the best illustration of this principle. I was hired to speak to twenty-two student leaders, called Texas Teen Ambassadors. Their job was to promote antismoking legislation and encourage their peers not to smoke or to quit smoking. Talk about giving to others! These kids were putting themselves out there for the good of others in a big way. I thought I was going the extra mile teaching these students what it meant to be a real leader. But then I met Kim, the waitress at our hotel.

The first night, the students and I ate in the hotel restaurant. Kim, a petite Asian woman, wore the biggest smile I had ever seen. She buzzed around throughout dinner taking care of us, and I saw how this lady was on *FIRE* for others. She treated the students as if they were highly paid executives. We asked for extra rolls and she ensured they were fresh out of the oven! She refilled our tea and water, and wore that same big smile while doing so. Our preordered meal included lemon pie for dessert, but Kim also brought us a complimentary batch of hot chocolate chip cookies made especially for us! The students and I were ***FIRED UP***!

I asked Kim about getting some milk to accompany our cookies. She told me that milk was normally $1.60 per person. I told her I would be happy to pay for it. She brought out a tray of milk and told us that the restaurant usually charges for milk, but that today it was FREE! We all cheered and clapped for Kim—and as we were leaving, I saw students hugging her and showing their gratitude. I was blown away!

Paying It Forward with Kindness

The power of kindness inspires others to display future acts of kindness.

Two days later, the student ambassador training ended. I was sharing my last words of wisdom with the students when the doors burst open and in walked Kim holding—you guessed it—a batch of hot cookies and cold milk. Kim received a standing ovation from the students! FOR COOKIES! When the room settled, I asked Kim to join me at the front of the room. I told her that it was my job to teach these students how to care about others, but that she truly demonstrated it with her actions, infectious smile, and heartfelt actions for us all. I asked her, "Would you share why you love your job so much? What inspires you to be so kind to us?"

She paused, smiled, and simply said, "It is my pleasure to serve you." Let that sink in. She gets pleasure from giving, and as she gives it, it returns to her in various ways. Some may say that is cultural or that it is just a trait within the hospitality industry. I think it's more than that.

Living the Golden Rule

No matter what business we are in, we are in the people business. When we make others feel important, appreciated, and recognized, and when we go the extra mile, we understand the true meaning of being FIRED UP! Being fired up is about *UNDERSTANDING* that your life, your job, your position, and your mission is about *serving others*. Some call it servant leadership. Think about it. How can you help someone if you don't understand and serve them?

Kim understood that these twenty-two students were without their families in a city far from home, staying in a hotel for perhaps the first time, and participating in leadership training all day. She knew intuitively that a big smile, lots of kindness and nurturing—and of course cookies, like any great mom would bake for her kids—would make them feel welcome and at home. She didn't get paid to provide that. But I'm betting she cleaned up in tips. If you truly want to make a difference in your company, with your clients, in your organization, in your community, with your co-workers, and with everyone else in your life, then put yourself in those people's shoes and consider how you might want to be treated. Then do those very things to create that service.

Consider for one moment that the guy who cut you off in traffic might be late to work. If he didn't hit you, LET IT GO. Consider that the person answering your customer service call may be going through a divorce, fighting for her kids, or having a few personal challenges. Consider the co-worker whom you despise. He or she might have problems beyond your knowledge, and might need you to cut him or her a little slack so you both can get through the day in peace. Life is difficult enough without introducing hostility toward one another. We all have issues, challenges, and personality defects that make us a little nutty at times. I find that if I try to take another person's perspective before reacting, I have a better chance of relating and connecting, and often have a better outcome. Maya Angelou once said, "I've learned that people will forget what you said, people will forget what you did, but people will never forget how you made them feel." When you act with kindness, it's your gift to the world—and it makes the world of the person receiving your kindness a little bit brighter. Don't you want in on that?

Think about every grievance you have ever had. How often did you try to take in the other person's perspective before letting him or her have it? Every time I pause and think about the other person's point of view before I respond, things usually go smoothly. I have to think about what my assistant may be feeling or dealing with before I discus what I want done. I have to think about my clients' perspective and expectations when preparing for their events. I have to consider what my parents are going through at this time of their lives and demonstrate patience and understanding. I have to do the same with my friends as well. When I come from that place of understanding, I feel peace and control.

As a result of implementing this in my life, I now view difficult situations, which used to bring out the worst in me, as opportunities to practice being my best. Who needs your understanding? Whose perspective do you need to better understand?

I can't guarantee that you will get a raise, move up the corporate ladder, or get a pat on the back for doing any of these things. There will be times when people will treat you with love and give you the same understanding you give them, and there will be times when they won't. But you will feel a whole lot better and cause a lot less damage if you take the high road of understanding and focus on being a good, kind, giving, and caring person. It is my experience that things usually go pretty well when I practice understanding—especially when I don't expect anything in return.

So keep your intentions in check. Work to UNDERSTAND, and you'll be FIRED UP!

FIRED UP and Doing Something About It! Step #6

1. Challenge yourself to smile at every person you come across today and reflect on the reaction you receive.
2. Learn the names of the people you interact and work with. Call them by name and see if you notice a difference in how the interactions go.
3. Make a list of people in your life that you are related to, work for, work with, or anyone in general with whom you regularly cross paths; or someone you are holding a grievance against or with whom you may be upset. Then hypothetically walk in these people's shoes.

What might they be going through? Write about it. If you are led to call or speak to some of them, do so with understanding and kindness.

4. Write a note or make a call to anyone to whom you want to show appreciation, care, or concern. Apologize and ask forgiveness from those whom you have wronged. Understand that *what you do matters*, not just to yourself, but also to those around you. Be kind. It really does take a village to make the world a better, more FIRED UP place to live and work.

Chapter 7

PRESENT: Live Here and Now

Have you ever contemplated death? My favorite chapter of *The Untethered Soul* asks the reader to contemplate death. Singer states that, "Death is our greatest teacher." His words resonate with me. I am learning that if you want to know how to live, you should try thinking about your pending death. Life is so precious, yet we waste it by worrying, being afraid, procrastinating, watching countless hours of television and movies, or obsessing about our body's imperfections. We miss out on life because we waste it thinking about things we can't control or that don't even matter. We forget to live because we forget how easily we could die.

Take a moment now and contemplate your death.

Yesterday Is History—Tomorrow Is a Mystery: All You Have Is the Present

Now start worrying about something trivial like why your girlfriend hasn't returned your call or all the things on your to-do list. Which of these are really important? Think about dying tomorrow and then locate all your fears and resentments. Where are they now? Gone! Forgotten! Petty grievances fly away when you contemplate death. All we have is the present. Author Bill Keane said it well: "Yesterday is history, tomorrow is a mystery, today is a gift from God, which is why we call it the present." Enjoy the PRESENT now. Be PRESENT in the moment and in everything you do. Get FIRED UP about it!

Do you want to waste another moment worrying about what happened yesterday? How much fun are you having when you worry about what might or might not happen tomorrow? If you were going to die today, would you spend all day writing emails, surfing the net, or reading Facebook updates? Would you read a tabloid magazine all day? Would you complain about the weather? Would you get upset at your child, your friend, your spouse, or your co-workers? How about that disgruntled customer? If today was your last day on earth, would you let a customer's petty grievance over a measly $2 get the best of you? NO! You might smile and laugh and gladly try to meet her needs by giving her two of your own dollars just to see how she reacts.

If you knew that today was your last day alive, what would you say to the people you love or work with—or those you serve at your work, school, or organization? Would you take the time to compliment them, or write them little notes of gratitude, or give them small signs of how much they have meant to you? *What are you waiting for?* Why not start NOW? How many times have you heard people say things, like, "Don't work too hard! Take it easy! Don't take life so seriously!" When we hear these statements, we know that the people saying them are showing they care about us. But perhaps they are being unrealistic about what we actually are confronting in the moment. They don't always exactly understand how sometimes we have to power through to get the job done, reach the end result, or finish a task that will have a long-lasting impact on our lives. Sometimes we just have to work hard, but then we can relish in our accomplishments with the people we love the most by being PRESENT. If we were PRESENT to begin with, then those things would happen automatically in most cases.

We should be serious about treating our customers with kindness and support. We should take our mission to serve and give excellent service seriously. Doing so is not always easy, but it is always worth it. People who are FIRED UP push themselves to be their best! They make the most of the moment. If someone says to you, "You didn't have to do that!" or, "That is awfully thoughtful; you put forward way too much effort and trouble!" your response should be, "Yes, but you are worth it!" or, "It was truly my pleasure and I would do it again!"

Leave Your Soul Print

As I am writing this chapter, it is well past midnight. I have to meet my deadline. I'll have completed this book in five days! I couldn't have done it without a lot of help, though. My team is FIRED UP too! They are up late with me from coast to coast. My editors are on the East and West Coasts and they are up too, working away. We have been writing and editing non-stop for three days to get this book done. Why is this so important to get done on time? I may not live to see tomorrow—who really knows?—and I want my truths in print and accessible to others who also want to be FIRED UP! My life has meaning and purpose and so does yours! I may be ashes tomorrow but my spirit will live on. My good friend and best-selling author and speaker Anne Bruce calls it leaving your soul print on earth. This book is part of my personal soul print. What's yours?

I want people to know I was here! I did something and it was great! When you pass on and a loved one delivers your eulogy, do you want him or her to say you loved the Dallas Cowboys and your favorite television show was *Seinfeld*? Maybe you do—maybe you poured your heart, soul, and allegiance into those passions. Then what you are really being honored for is not the TV show or the team, but your passion, loyalty, support, lust for life, and competitive spirit. Now there's a legacy to admire!

Sobering Consequences of Being Distracted

How do we stay in the present with all of the distractions we face in today's modern society? With televisions, computers, cell phones, iPods, and countless other gadgets and games distracting us 24/7, very few of us are ever really in the moment. In 2010, there were 3,000 deaths and more than 400,000 injuries due to distracted driving.[2] And more than 1,100 pedestrians went to the emergency room with injuries received while using their cell phones while walking.[3] Being distracted can kill you—and who really wants today to be his or her last day? Get in the moment! I confess to talking while driving or texting while walking. I too have to remind myself to be in the moment! I am encouraging myself as much as I am encouraging you. Live in the now as you drive, jog, or just walk across the street. Not doing so could put you in the hospital! As Ferris Bueller said in the movie *Ferris Bueller's Day Off*, "Life moves pretty fast. If you don't stop and look around once in a while, you could miss it!"

Get in the moment, then do your best to stay there for a while. BE PRESENT, and experience how your true purpose and your true passion rises within you. Now you can really start living a FIRED UP LIFE! Because it's palpable. When we are present, we become capable of hearing the greater, deeper voice within. This requires silence. Be quiet. Don't wait for your turn to talk next. Just listen.

Silence is an activator for all great things, because it requires contemplation and collaboration with something bigger than ourselves—

---

2 http://www.distraction.gov.
3 "Dangers of Distracted Driving Growing," *Daily Herald*, July 31, 2012, http://www.dailyherald.com/article/20120730/news/707309896/.

our God, Source, Eternal Energy, love, joy and inner peace. When we calibrate being present with our inner voice, we not only experience greater happiness, but we get the answers we've been looking for and the solutions to many of our challenges and questions. Being in the moment is powerful and can reap great returns.

So how do we do it? Follow these simple steps in this order, and they will work every time.

FIRED UP and Doing Something About It! Step #7

Step 1. STOP. Just simply stop what you are doing. Think before you speak. You'll sound more intelligent if you do.

Step 2. BREATHE. Feel and be aware of your breath going in and out. This practice is part of Vipassana Meditation. Vipassana means seeing things as they really are. Observe your breath for two minutes, and watch how much more present and aware you become.

Step 3. Be in the PRESENT MOMENT. Be totally focused on whatever you are doing *when you are doing it*. Carefully and slowly move through your daily routine with focus and clarity. Take your time. Chew, enjoy, and taste your food. Do one thing at a time. Turn off your phone when driving. Look at yourself in the mirror and smile. Let peace resonate within you! You are wonderful. Enjoy you, enjoy your life, enjoy what you get to do with it today. BE FIRED UP ABOUT IT!

Step 4. Contemplate the Circle of Life—from birth to death and beyond. To every season there is a reason. What is your reason to be present today?

The personal growth and learning begins after you've completed reading this book. Immediately start your own FIRED UP! JOURNAL. Post your thoughts, musings, and insights on our website and through social media. We want to know how you are taking the FIRED UP! concept to the next level of learning and growing in your life. Your stories, input, and creative ideas might just wind up in one of our upcoming FIRED UP! books from the series being created now.

Being a part of your journey has been my distinct pleasure. I look forward to hearing from you and to remaining FIRED UP with you for life! I'm proud to be part of your organization's team. I look forward to hearing from you soon!

Conclusion

Way to go! You did it! Are you FIRED UP? If not, go back and reread the book! It's actually not a bad idea, considering we must saturate our minds with these ideas to the point where they become second nature.

Okay, let's go through the list together. Remember to ask yourself each day:

- What is my FUEL level today?
- What does my INVENTORY look like today? How can I use my strengths today? What should I let go of?
- How can I REFRAME this situation or opportunity?
- What is my ENERGY plan for today?
- Today I DECLARE that I am… and I will…!
- Who and What need my UNDERSTANDING today? Can I see his or her point of view?
- Today I will be PRESENT. I will stop to breathe. I will live in the moment!

Are you ready to BE FIRED UP for today and for the rest of your life?

Fired Up in Action

These principles really do work. The love of my life and I recently hiked Angel's Landing in Utah's Zion National Park. Our friends and loved ones kept saying we had to do it and that it would be a great experience for us to share. The weather on the day we did the hike was very warm. We started to hesitate and began making excuses—it's so hot, we can do it another time, we are both afraid of heights. But then we said, "Hey, we are here! Let's not back out now! Let's get FIRED UP about it!"

Getting Fired Up Means Facing Down Your Fears!
So we started hiking and talking through the FIRED UP steps as we climbed: *What FUELS our fire? Well, we want to share this experience with one another and overcome our fear of heights. What a great opportunity to do this together! What is our INVENTORY? We are strong and healthy, we have each other should something go awry, and if we need to stop and rest, we will. We have hiked up mountains before. We have looked down from tall buildings before. We will be fine! Let's REFRAME this situation. This is going to be FUN! The view from the top is going to be incredible. This will be an experience we will never forget and it will form a bond between us as well. Let's keep our ENERGY up by drinking plenty of water, eating protein bars, and resting when we need to along the way. We DECLARE that we are going to the TOP of Angel's landing! We have what it takes and there is no stopping us! We UNDERSTAND that we both have a bit of anxiety and fear about doing this, but that is just human. That is okay. We will be patient with each other, take our time, and encourage each other all along the way. Let's be totally PRESENT, keep breathing, stay in the moment, and enjoy every step along this path. If we take it one step at a time, we will get to the top. We made it! The view at the top is so beautiful. It feels like God put a mountain here just for us to climb so we could shift our perspectives on the landscape of life just perfectly.*

We were so FIRED UP during the climb that the time flew by and we enjoyed every minute. The heat and our stamina were never factors and the view from 5,785 feet was pretty darn sweet!

What is your mountain? If you believe you can reach the top, then you can! So what are you waiting for? Get FIRED UP and start climbing! Earlier I mentioned Zig Ziglar's book *See You at the Top*—it's so appropriately named. I believed him then and I believe him now. I'll be seeing you at the top, my friend.

Let's Continue this Journey Together at FiredUpEmployees.com!

Be sure to visit my website at FiredUpEmployees.com today! And tell your friends about it. Right there, you will find all of our social media links. Be sure to post your thoughts about this book on all the social media outlets you like best, and write to me personally about how you used this book to better your life, your workplace, and your personal journey with friends and family. I look forward to reading your posts on Facebook, LinkedIn, Twitter, and others. I want my fans and audiences to share in your insights and thoughts about how you used this book's FIRED UP tips and tools to take you to the top. By going to FiredUpEmployees.com, I can be right by your side, every step of the way! This is going to be awesome. I appreciate your collaboration, so let's stay FIRED UP together!

So Where Do We Go from Here?

Our next stop on the journey will be my global FIRED UP! Project and television series/reality show—I'll be taking you from Boston to Bosnia, Dallas to Dubai, San Antonio to Singapore. Our FIRED UP TEAM is growing worldwide—we pride ourselves on being a global organization. We will be posting all of our global initiatives as they roll out, and we'll want you on board! We'll not only see you at the top, but we'll see you on the other side of the world!